The Bones of the World
Begin to Show

The Bones of the World Begin to Show

Marilyn Gear Pilling

Black Moss Press

2009

Library and Archives Canada Cataloguing in Publication

Pilling, Marilyn Gear, 1945-

    The bones of the world begin to show / Marilyn Gear Pilling.

Poems.

ISBN 978-0-88753-458-4

    I. Title.

PS8581.I365 B65 2009   C811'.54   C2009-901327-4

Cover photo by Marty Gervais

Published by Black Moss Press at 2450 Byng Road, Windsor, Ontario, N8W 3E8. Canada. Black Moss books are distributed in Canada and the U.S. by LitDistCo. All orders should be directed there.

Black Moss Press would like to acknowledge the support of the Canada Council for the Arts and the Ontario Arts Council for their support of its publishing program.

ONTARIO ARTS COUNCIL
CONSEIL DES ARTS DE L'ONTARIO

Le Conseil des Arts | The Canada Council
du Canada | for the Arts

Printed in Canada

This book is dedicated
with love and gratitude
to my sister Marie Gear Cerson
who from the day she was born
has made all the difference.

Conversation on a Budapest Bus, September 11, 2001

At home in Canada it is not yet dawn, and here, waiting
for a bus in the hills of Buda, my sister regrets the rain,
but it can rain toads for all I care; today, I am a nineteenth
century woman, in awe that yesterday I entered a heavy
machine and it rose in the sky and carried me here,
amazed that one week ago I worked the last day of a thirty
year career, and now am free. We find seats, rain pitters
on the windows, we breathe air suffused with the smell of
damp woolen coats, passengers gaze through streaming
panes at the blurred blue hills. *So what's this rooster thing?*
my sister asks, when I tell her my plan to look for a glass
bird, a souvenir of this journey. *The rooster appears on the
border between worlds,* I tell her. *That call. How it cracks open
the morning.*

Contents

The Sign

They're in the west field this year, he says.

Though we're in our fifties now, we climb over the gate
as we used to.

He leads the way, the farm now his home, the horses
his. My sister

follows. Though born first, I come last, watch them walk
single file up the path

the horses have made. The hill cuts the sky, a gentle, cupping
line of blue. Wind winnows

the long grass, bends it to echo the curving line of horizon.
Little brother, baby sister.

My eyes trace the long-familiar road of their backbones
exposed in this heat.

Late June, the farm a wild bride of neglected
beauty, our parents in their grave

seven years, long enough to remove most traces of their
husbandry.

As we climb, I wonder which of us will be the first
to follow them.

———

When we crest the hill, the horses look up, blow from soft oval
nostrils. The skin on their flanks

shudders under the flies. They surround us, all seven,
nose us, then Flo,

named for our mother, born on her birthday, shows long, worn
teeth, rips the silk scarf from my

body, renders it a rag.

The Sour Red Cherries

came ripe in July and their last week
on the tree was war.
My aunt was out there at dawn every morning
in her long white night-
gown, finger on the trigger,
one eye closed, mouth under her moustache
pressed tight. When she pulled
the trigger the unholy
racket scattered starlings and robins all over the sky,
caused the dog to lay his ears flat
to his head and howl, and the bay yearling
to thud to the back fence.

After breakfast, my aunt handed the rifle
to her daughter, scrubbed the sleepers from our eyes
and sent us to start our shift on two kitchen chairs
outside, guarding the cherries.
Marge's method was a cavalier fire
at the sky, rifle askew at arm's
length, pointed in any old
direction. We laughed behind our hands
when my aunt came out to demonstrate her squint,
her careful aim; the rifle was a toy, its only ammunition
the eschatological intensity of its explosion.

Many years later, in winter, my aunt died with one
cherry pie in the freezer. Marge and I
thawed the pie; while it warmed, we stood at the pantry
window, looked out at the shrouded bones
of tree, talked of searching
for the rifle, firing one last salute.
Instead, we sat up to the worn oilcloth
and ate half the pie each. Every bite exploded
sweet-sour summer in our mouths
and we scraped and scraped
our pink-flowered plates with our forks 'til they shrieked,
then stuck out our tongues and licked and licked
'til the china was wet with happiness.

The Night My Sister and Her Husband Babysat the Grandkids

The other two were in the bunk beds,
asleep: Brooklyn, long hair of spreading strawberry-gold,
Julia on stage, dancing under her eyelids.

                                       It was the third,
Gus, who cringed and cried as lightning spliced
the darkness and thunder boomed
judgement on the town.

                          They took him into the bedroom.
They took Gus into the master bedroom,
where sink and shower are scoured, where every piece
of underwear reposes in its own compartment
within the drawers, they took him into the master
bed with the fine, combed-cotton Egyptian
sheets. My sister and her husband
took this fat, elderly German shepherd named Gus
into their bed. His shedding his slavering his open mouth
his breath his black gums the gleam of his large yellow teeth
his blunt nails the dark cave of his ears his ineluctable
otherness.

                 Though their habit is to sleep
entwined, they put this creature the size of a small horse
between them. They settled his great head
on a pillow they'd fetched from the guest

---

bed, they laid their own bodies next to the barrel
tub of his torso, they breathed his slightly damp
coat, each placed a palm on his flank,
and the three of them slept.

Adam of Ayton

He moved in a nimbus of sun-scorched
dust, walked across the gravel parking lot
to find us, washed up as we were
on the dry shore of a Sunday afternoon

halfway between home and our journey's
end, time lolling out back in an old
tire that swung from the branch of an
apple tree. He knelt among us

on sharp stones, rolled under the van,
laid his hand on the oxygen sensor
before I'd even finished
my story: how the noise started

in Guelph, how just as we reached this
small town, Linda saw the engine light
come on, Ross checked the manual,
read aloud *See your Toyota dealer,*

and we watched our hopes run off
to look for windfalls under the apple tree.
It was only later, when I talked
to the brother – Adam himself lying

under our car, in a nimbus of sparks
this time – that I recognized the kind
of story we'd stumbled into, the child
who arrives in this world with a genius

that will drive his life. Our rescuer
had dismantled cars and trucks
from early childhood on,
restored complete with running

boards the Ford in the driveway
to its youthful '56 self, could listen
and touch and know within seconds
the heart of the mysteries

that stymied both the schooled and
the experienced. There's the other
story, too, the helpers who came from
behind the counter of the shabby store,

took our heaviness onto their own
backs, phoned 'til they found
a man who would search the sleeping
streets 'til he found the boy

who could fix anything; none of them
knew his name. Adam
tried to keep his work in the realm
of the gift, of course,

but the three of us
were from the other world;
we opened our wallets,
we pressed the twenties into his hands.

Royal Jelly

We bathed in succession in the same water,
me first, little brother, baby sister, mother,
father last. The order always the same,
the water clean and warm when I had my
bath, grey and tepid by the time
our father had his.
                    Once, I was remembering
this aloud, telling the story to my teenage
daughters in the presence of my mother.
My daughters squealed *Gross*,
one of them threw herself on the carpet
and windmilled her extremities, a white-limbed
octopus of distaste.
I said that it was strange
that I'd always gone first and my mother
said, *Oh no oh no not strange at all*
we always catered to you, you
were the Queen Bee in that household.
This was in the days when such truths offended
me, and I flushed and denied it
at which the octopus rose from the rug,
swept her mimicking self
across the room in a way that was
royal highnessy and unmistakably

me, and my mother shook like cubed Jell-O
at a family reunion, she and my daughters
laughed so hard their canines shone
and I wanted to kill them all.

                                That's as long ago
now as the serial bathing was then
and of course I'd give every jar of royal jelly
in the hive to see that Jell-O on the picnic table
again, how the faces of those ruby cubes
juggled the light.

A Knowledge Earned by Few

He rises from darkness, carried upward by the moving
stairs, standing neither straight nor slumped,
just there, scarf of red and long black coat, face familiar

from photos on dust jackets, the train already in a chuff
of moving on. This man
for whom she now unlocks her door is a danger

to himself but not to her. She knows that he has been
in every kind of darkness,
trespassed every boundary, paid the high price,

retched up his promises, seen himself trip on tin
legs into the gutter, that tonight
he will need a woman, any woman, and for this night

she wants to be that woman. She knows that he ate
what he was given in the underworld,
drank deeply, that when he emerged he looked back,

that he must return again and again, that he holds
in his body a knowledge
earned by few, a knowledge she can taste only

through the inchoate story of the mouth and the hands,
the buzz of blood, the sweet
grace notes of the body. Tomorrow she will take him

to the bus and when they part he will call her sweetheart,
for he will not remember
her name, and as he climbs the bus stairs, she will see

a woman reading in a window seat, and she will know
that when the light
turns green and the bus roars exhaust, he will sit down

beside that woman, that as the bus grinds into the future,
he will not look back,
that this – how else to say it – is meet and right.

The Words

Last night I dreamt of you, though these past
months I rarely think of you, and no longer
       miss you.

            I knew you
so well I could read your body and
       always your body
              told me
what your lips would never say. That almost invisible
stiffening of the muscles above
your clavicle that meant
I'd displeased you. How you took off your glasses
when I'd made you happy, laid them
on the table and let the light from the big windows
fill your hazel eyes, your voice at those times
cello-resonant.

         While you sat across from me
in the cafés, talking – and how you loved
to talk, to sculpt and polish and bronze
your ideas – I read the timbre of your voice,
studied the tilt of your head,
how you held
yourself, your posture the paradigm

mothers have in mind when they harangue
their children to straighten up.

                         I knew
                 that you loved me,
but when it came to love, I needed to hear
the words.

In the dream, I wished
            it could have been enough –
your glasses on the table,
the light in your hazel eyes,
the alto notes
                 rich and round,
        filling slowly with wine.

The Triangle

I've just handed the friend I've loved for a decade a new
   poem. Already I regret this, for she is reading it
      with that expression her face assumes when she

opens a menu. Tempt me. Woo me. I'm nothing if not
   discriminating. The three of us sip our red
      wine; Leah and I wait for Emmeline to speak.

The orange trumpets that once bloomed on the vine
   that forms the roof over our heads have dropped,
      shriveled to slippery brown stains that may

cause a fall if you're not careful where you step.
   The triangle formed by our chairs is the right-
      angled sort loved by teachers of geometry.

Emmeline does speak, finally, about the poem, which is
   about a woman gorging herself on peas in the pod.
      She says that I should not say that my father

once did this too, that bringing in my father is irrelevant.
   I say that it is not my father, it is the narrator's
      father, Leah says that she is by no means sure

that the line should come out, I say that the line is my
   favourite in the poem, Emmeline's face says
      that there is not one thing on the menu that

interests her. The skull drops from above, hits the deck
   with a sharp rap precisely midpoint on the hypotenuse
      that runs between Emmeline and me.

The three of us exclaim, look up, see only the familiar
   tangle of vine that rests on the pergola. I take
      the skull between thumb and one finger,

we consider whether it is a cat or a squirrel, even a rat.
   We inspect the skull from all angles. Silently
      I note that the long yellow teeth are intact.

Failure

All that womanly elegance, and what I remember
most clearly now
                              is the part that didn't seem to fit
with the rest of you – your hands. Those big,
broad hands, fat blue ridges on their backs,
              the fingers that widened at the tip,
your hands, so at odds with the silver rings
              with which you adorned them.

Long before I began to back away, I'd read
the chapters of your need
              of me, inscribed in the proud
cords of your neck. As always,
              I thought I was
                        or could be
who the other person needed.
                                        As always,
I failed.

I'm remembering that day.
                        The day
your hands threw stones at my windows. Clods of dirt,
a spray of gravel. Back windows, front, then back
again. Sharp rap of keys on glass.

               I lay curled, clothed,
in the empty bathtub, shower curtain closed, a knock
in my chest, afraid you'd mount the ladder,
      find me
in an upstairs room.
Me, as crazy as you
          by then.

As always,
        I ended up running away.
Even now, when I think of you, you're behind me
       flying low, your hands huge,
           spatulate fingers
                 extended.

Tracing the Cracks

The rest of us have never travelled these roads
   so Lucy brings a mannequin up from
her basement, dresses her in a long green
   coat of brushed wool, leans her
against the mailbox. We are to look for her
   instead of guessing at landmarks.
When I see her, I brake, and drive in the lane

to the farmhouse where women – two artists,
   three writers have gathered to talk about art
and the female body. Such a grand subject.
   Probably inevitable we wouldn't
live up to it. In truth, we talk about our hair.
   And we talk about men. About ourselves,
in relation to men. Lucy asks whether we've

ever faked an orgasm. Two of us have faked none.
   Two of us seem not to have heard the question.
One of us has faked four hundred and ninety-
   seven orgasms. Says she kept track. One of us
has never had an orgasm. Says she doesn't care.
   Sheila starts talking about her sister,
whose husband just left her for another woman.

Her sister's weeping. How the cry came
　　from a place deeper than Sheila had known
existed. I tell about two women who left
　　work and came to my home and heard and
held me, in the same situation. Anne: the father
　　of her four children told her years
later that he left because her journeys

inner and outer called up his mother, who left
　　when he was a small boy. I talk about my
sister. How I want my bones to lie with hers
　　for eternity. Anne says she never got over
the loss of her sister. Sheila talks
　　about her students. Says all the young
women she knows who cut themselves come

from homes where the mother's boyfriend,
　　an uncle, some man, had sex with them.
On and on we go, story after story.
　　That night, Lucy walks down the long dark
lane, brings the mannequin into the house.
　　There are deep cracks on the back
of her head. All of us bend to look and touch

and trace the cracks. Lucy says there's a
    sport in these parts, young men with baseball
bats who speed by in pickup trucks,
    lean out and bash the heads off mailboxes.
Lucy says it's a miracle our woman still
    has her head. She says she'll give her
a space of her own in the attic.

Lucy says, *She is one of us now.*

To Know Him

She's been telling him that it was winter when she left home
yesterday afternoon – sleet, wind bringing down branches,
dark churn of sky – yet here, in his city only three hours
southwest of hers, it's still autumn, a light

turned on inside the golden beeches, translucent yellow
maples, leaves of the burning bush in their last days a dark-
red. She's been teasing him, telling him it's always
warm and sunny where he lives and he says

that as he drove to work this morning, he wondered at
the day's glory, then remembered that the woman who brings
the sun was coming. Several times today, as they've
walked about the campus, he has stepped out

a few paces ahead, avid as always for what's next, and each
time her attention is caught by something in his gait,
something seen from behind, each time she struggles
with the language of his body as one struggles

to remember a name – effort, a little moth flit of almost
getting it, effort, another moth flit – this, one more
piece of the puzzle in her attempt to know him.
As she drove yesterday to his city, the sky

---

rolled away the clouds and stepped out washed in tender silk,
a pale half moon high on its left shoulder. She watched
    the slow flush of sky, the shadows stretching
        themselves across the stubbled fields,

listened over and over to Donald Hall read *Kicking the Leaves*
a life in leaves, the poem coming round again and again
    to this space between autumn and winter; she watched
        the birds swirl in the sky like flocks of leaves

kicked high, felt the pieces of her life swirl with them,
then tarot to earth, each time in a different order.
    She's known him for four years this month,
        has heard his stories of the family he's created,

always a new story, the heart of each the same – a fillip
of delight at the nature of each life. All day she watches
    him, the short direct flights of him from person to person,
        one day in a long life of connecting,

alighting for brief moments of intimacy, a life of threading
invisible songlines among others. When they leave the library,
    he does it again, steps ahead into the shifting tints
        of late afternoon, and the moth flits so close

that she knows it will land this time. Is it the way his shoe meets
the ground, is it the slight spring of his body, the strong sapling
    in it, how you can still see the young man? Is it
        the slight swing, not swagger, not quite

insouciance, the way the soles of his feet connect with the earth,
the angle maybe…ah, here it is – given. No one owns this man,
not even a little piece of him, his feet are at home
wherever he is, and not only that, in each

moment he sheds the one before. She remembers Arundhati Roy,
nuclear war a threat, a journalist asking why she didn't leave
India, Roy's reply, *where would I go, how would I live*
if every friend, every tree, every home, every dog,

squirrel and bird was destroyed, who would I love, who would
love me back? She'd thought, then – yes, we'd all feel that way –
yet now, walking ahead of her through maple leaves
fallen and falling is a man who could survive that.

They hug goodbye and she moves towards her car through
a light deep with motes of dust, deep with earth cooling
and returning its stores of heat, and she kicks the leaves
a little, watches them fall, looks to see

which of the major arcana is up this time, and yes, sure,
half-hidden by a scrum of gold and red – the Magician.
She looks back when she reaches her car,
though she knows he's gone, feels a pang that's

almost guilt, as if a door marked private had opened
as she passed, and she'd looked in
when she should, perhaps,
have walked on by.

Guestdom

At six in the morning you find her in short
nightgown and knee socks, cooking the potatoes
　　　you forgot to serve for dinner
the night before. She found them herself – potatoes, eggs, the cast
iron frying pan your children say belongs
in a museum. She opened the door of the oven
you haven't cleaned in years.
　　　　　　　　　　She offers you
breakfast. Too early, you croak, shuffle forward to move
dirty wine glasses out of her way,
and drop a goblet
　　　　　　　　beside her big toe
where it shatters,
dramatically,
strands her,
on an island surrounded by crystal shards.
　　　　　　　　　　　　She turns off
the burner, reaches for your hands, you half-lift her
to shore, off she goes to armour herself
in jeans and blouse and shoes, especially
the shoes.
　　　　　　You tell all your guests to make themselves
at home, and you mean it, you tell them
the contents of fridge and cupboard

are theirs, but they sit like ducks frozen
to the ice wherever you happen
to put them first and when they've gone, you find
even the small comforts you set out for them
undisturbed.
                    You believe – don't you? – that there's a place
on this planet for the frozen ducks **and** the maniac
who finds your forgotten
potatoes, a place, too, for every shade between,
so off you go
                    you follow her, you want to observe
this rare form of guestdom.

          She opens every closed
door on the second floor. Discovers the linen
closet, mismatched
sheets and threadbare towels. She finds
the attic, looks up the stairs.
                    Will she mount them, will she
drag open the crawl space door, haul out
the boxes, find the diary
you kept in grade nine, discover how much you wanted sex
with Mr. Schmidt?
                    She places a foot on the first
step. Undisturbed for years, the original red shag carpet
stirs at her tread, it sighs
an easeful incurious dust into her eyes.

———

The Silent Body of the Lake

i. Bookends

The world dropped iron bookends at either end of our
retreat.
      And yet,
when we had tunneled through snow and deep cold
to the cottage door, when Linda had made
the fire and I had laid the salmon to grill, when you had
opened the red wine and Ross had
unpacked the books, when we'd settled
where we could see the white
lake frozen to the sky and hear the wind drive
ice against our panes,
we found ourselves in the same book we wrote
the first time we four found our way
to these pages where before and after
are not, only
the cold the fire the wind the hard stars the red wine
the words on the page.
      One night,
Linda plays the music she's chosen for this week,
and around midnight you ask her to play
again your favourite, the one
in which some of the intervals
          between notes

are so close the notes are almost
indistinguishable.
                    Still later,
Linda and Ross tie on snowshoes, open the door to sub-zero
cold, clump down the slope
to the vast body of ice and set off into distance.
You and I in the fire's warmth
speak of the deep pleasure of consonance in the sounds
you asked to have replayed,
preceded and followed as they are
by dissonance,
how the sounds approach that place where opposites so called
– life and death for instance –
turn into one another.
The last log trembles, rains sparks, gives up
rings of its life to the ashes.
We wait in the warmth
for the shush of returning shoes on snow.

ii. Black Ice

After the morning of work and discussion, we walk
   outside in the cold and as we round the bend
in the road that reveals the frozen lake, the extreme
   of white, the thin black line of open
water at the furthest point of vision,
   you say that last evening as we sat
side by side on the couch, watching the film
   on the writer Denton Welch, you fell asleep, deeply
asleep, just as the film showed the event
   that changed the writer's life.

                        We move towards
the white lake, our feet struggle for traction
   on the ice beneath the snow; on the slope
of the last bank you take my arm, and even through
   my heavy coat I feel your touch
as warmth. You say that when you awoke
   you saw the unfamiliar room, the film,
the blond hair of the woman beside you, and you
   knew that she was not your wife, and you
did not know where you were, or who she was,
   or what you were doing there, and for as long as
ten seconds your mind scrabbled, it slipped and
   slipped on the black ice of unknowing;
there was not one thing to hold onto.

40

iii. Sofia

The only true wisdom lives far from mankind, out in the great
loneliness, and can be reached only through suffering.

> Igjugarjuk

Early mornings, I tiptoe to the edge of the loft,
look out upon the silent body
of the lake.
>   Silver ridges of ice to the horizon,
>   sheen of pearl sky. No sign
of Huron restless beneath.
>   The light
white, extreme. The same, perhaps, that opened before
Saul on the road to Damascus.

Below on the mattress Ross sleeps, his upturned face
serene. You are silent behind the third
bedroom door. In the kitchen,
>   Linda grinds the coffee.

The white sun moves the day
>   as slowly as we please
>   across the sky.

Maple table, pens and papers, cups of coffee, notebooks.
>   A net of meaning, silken draglines that connect us.
>   Evenings, the fire.

41

It's only later, when we've gone home and you've picked up
your life and seen it break apart
in your hands
that I remember how we returned

                                            again and again
to the window to gaze. Those unexpected holes
on the ice that opened to black
water. The footing, sharp and uncertain.
The relentless wind. Not knowing where the ice
would end, the sky begin.

You've set off now.
I'll watch until the whiteness takes you.

Far from humankind, your consolation prize
waits beneath her ice-bright,
rounded, dome.
                    Sofia.
I think that she has never seemed
more devoutly
            undesirable.

Month of My 60th Birthday

November arrived yesterday.

She ripped catalpa's big gold hearts from their fall show,
smashed them against my pane.

She rolled a sag-faced jack-o'-lantern down the road.

She blew the blue jay's feathers inside out,
blew them 'til he picked his way into the thickest tangle
of trumpet vine, clung there and fluffed.

All night she wept on the lip of the eaves trough.

All night she sighed in the fir tree, her whisper
liminal, tapped again and again
on the glass, summoned me
to the surface of sleep.

This morning, she has placed plump rain buds
in rows upon my storm window;
they wobble and refract dense light,
create of the garden a pointillist scene.

I move to the other window and look west –
blue distances not visible 'til now.

The bones of the world begin to show.

———

The Accident

Last week, Ross told me the story that pulsed with the sweet
handprints of his own
quick-flashing life
and this week he tells me how it was told to him
by the woman at the body
shop, who, when he appeared before her and said his name,
started as if she'd seen
a spirit, showed him
the wrecked car that was his, told him
the version the other
survivors had told
her, the stranger that was
himself, strapped to a board, gurney'd
to the ambulance, the mask,
the blood writing a river in his wake.

                        It's the wash of his
stories I hear, the grate of small stones, plash of currents.
He pivots his chair sideways
to mine. Now it's the wounded eye
I see, the crisscross of stitches beneath its black brow,
how its white has changed from milk
to blood, and haunting its center, the sliver of time
that came between him and his death.

                     Where will it take him,
this eye, I wonder – will it ever allow him
to turn
        the battered bowl of his face to the sun?

———

Loblaws, Easter Saturday

He came through the door marked *Staff,*
the creature hoisted on his shoulder, he opened
the glass case with his free hand & laid
his burden on its side among the pork loins
and stuffed boneless chicken. His head almost
in the case, he fussed with the limbs,
placed them just so on crushed ice; the front legs
were longer than a side of ribs.
*What's **that**?* I asked,
for the creature, though in one piece, had no head,
no feet, no innards, no skin, nothing by which
to identify it. *Dog,* he said, without missing
a beat. *Why, of course,* I shot back, *golden retriever,*
unmistakably. The other woman
at the case wheeled & ramrodded away &
we laughed & laughed & the real butcher came out &
I told him & he said to his Saturday part-
timer, *You shouldn't say that, some people might*
believe you, & we laughed again &
exchanged a look & I thought –
this, just this, in another life,
could be
the start of something.
Five minutes later, I was in the car beside
my husband, Easter turkey on ice

---

in the trunk. We'd argued that morning, & I looked
at him, neck stretched forward,
looking left, looking right, trying to pull onto the road,
& I thought of the lamb in the case, wondered
if it had seen
even the glint of the blade.

Before Pathology

The evening of the day I heard
that the pathology
was clear & he was going to live
after all
I prepared a special dinner
yes I chopped
red & green & yellow & orange
peppers slivered zucchini & walnuts
softened garlic on low sliced the Greek
feta I'd bought at the Lebanese
grocery I'd never been in before
but had entered
on the half-mile walk
from his hospital bed to my car
& prepared as I say a splendid
feast & opened
the Veuve Clicquot & poured it into my best
glass & opened as well with my bum
the back door & successfully
descended stairs
holding plate & best glass & fork & knife
& when most of my dinner then
spun off the plate & landed
in dirt yes yellow & orange peppers & all the chicken
face down in dirt

I laughed yes
laughed & thought of my old
self of the days before pathology
who would have stamped & sworn & cursed God who she
didn't believe in
anyway.

Vigil

That afternoon I made tea and we left the men for a time,
went to sit quietly in my room where she admired
the saffron and orange-red afghans
against the long blue sofa. We gazed
at the pale January sky my window revealed
and remembered together
that it was almost thirty years since she'd stayed
here to have her first baby, and she said
that sometimes now she feels
two hundred years old.
                        She began to tell me
about the books of her mother's she'd saved, how they
occupy two shelves in her own study now,
all of them by Mary Baker Eddy;
they were her mother's
Bible, she said.
                    I asked her to tell me her mother's
beliefs and the creed entire sighed itself
through her lips and I felt
its breath, its blood, the rise and fall of it, saw the fog
in her grey-blue eyes: *Matter does not exist.*
Only the metaphysical is real.
                        Even now, she said,
her mother long gone, she feels any sickness
as failure of spirit.

———

49

I picked up the saffron blanket
and covered our knees. She said that her brother
had died this past fall,
that she'd spent a lot of time with him. She leaned
her two hundred years against me and
described her long autumn vigil, the terrible swelling power
of matter as it dragged her own flesh and blood

      into the grave.

Theresa Tells Me a Story about Her Aunt

The doctor says she won't be discharged
     'til Monday, but Cora Mae wants to go
to the Baptist church on Sunday
where the old will walk down the aisle and be honoured.
     Ninety-four years, spine of a flagpole.

     Theresa offers to bring in her clothes,
asks her aunt if she knows what she wants to wear.
     Oh yes, says Cora Mae, on her face
the light of the first morning: *The pink suit, dear,*
not the petal-pink, the fiesta-pink voile;
it hangs beside the ivory lace chambray.
     The cream blouse with the tiny pink
carnations, the one with the darts, you know
     darts, do you dear?
               And the small white
dove of her hand reaches over,
forms one slowly diminishing pleat in Theresa's sleeve.

Theresa shakes her head, looks into my eyes.
     You know, when I got home,
I worried that it was a sin – Cora Mae's
vanity, her obsession with clothes.

———

I think of Chekhov, a century ago, dying in the spa
of Badenweiler, his letters home, his last letter
      to anyone, his last written words –
There is not a single decently dressed…woman.
      The lack of taste makes one depressed.

Cora Mae: *I'd like a pair of silk stockings and my girdle.*
I can ease the stockings over these bandages on my legs,
      don't you think, dear?

The Badenweiler spa. Arm in arm, they stroll the long
path lined with plane trees. Chekhov and Cora Mae.
      Her elegant head nodding assent, as he remarks
that of course the realm is aesthetics,
      not ethics.
                  Away from the buildings,
down the path, towards the woods. Disappearing into the mist.
      The fiesta-pink blur of her,
            his arm, moving to encircle her waist.

Solo

A few days before you died you asked me to sing
The Fairies Make Their Counterpanes as I'd sung it
at age nine for the Kiwanis Festival. The hospital
bed had been rolled up so you could sit to sleep,

for that was the only way you could breathe.
Pillows surrounded you, you looked like a white
queen in a bed of clouds, and though I could no longer
sing, I obeyed your command. You asked me

to stand, to cup one hand inside the other as I'd been
trained to do all those years ago by Mr. Attridge
who came to class three times a week and blew
the opening note on his pitch pipe. Every night,

you put my sister in the playpen beside the piano,
sat down and struck the opening A, then played
the accompaniment, just as Mr. Attridge played it
at school. The song was in the key of G, which means

that F is sharp, but the composer had (perversely)
made one of the F's natural, and I faltered every time
that F natural approached. You isolated the line,
had me sing it over and over and over, 'til my father

ciphering in the kitchen and my brother playing at his
feet wished on the composer an evil fate. When I stood
at the end of your hospital bed and cupped my right
hand inside my left and began in a cracked soprano

to sing *The fairies make their counterpanes from li-ttle
ti-ny threads,* my sister began to cry and my brother,
who was sitting by the window in the only easy chair,
got up and went into the hall. My sister thrust back

the white sheet and the blue counterpane and got into bed
with you and pulled the covers up to her chin. You said,
Get up out of that; what if the nurse comes in!
(for my sister was a doctor in that hospital), and my sister

pulled the covers right over her head. You told me
to begin again and you sang a whispery A to start me off
properly. I began, and as I sang of threads and elves and
heather-bells, I thought how the F natural had entered family

lore, how "hitting the F natural" had become a metaphor
known only to those who'd been in that small house
with the Grandma Moses drapes on the picture window
on those winter evenings of 1954, and as I faltered

towards the note for what was surely the last time,
my heart saw us with a clarity that was unsought –
my sister in bed beside you, my brother, visible, but more
in the hall than the doorway, my father, a mile down the

road in the nursing home six weeks from his own death,
you, the white queen with the blue tinge on her lips,
and me, reluctant soloist headed for some limbo
between F natural and F sharp – and I thought

how the skein that held us had thinned to flimsiest gossamer,
how the merest breath would take it,
how intricate its weave as it floated away,
how outrageous its unraveling.

At Last the Apple

Here, in the nursing home, the sun forms a golden
sword upon your blue spread.
The chair beside your bed is empty.
For ten years, our mother sat here,
witness to the disappearance
of your speech, your movement, your mind,
and these last months, your ability
to swallow. Now,
you are coughing, though you cannot
cough, struggling,
though you cannot
struggle. Your hair, still blond and darkly
matted to your head, your
breath tearing the silent air.
You are alone.
It is clear in an instant that I cannot merely visit you.
Clear that I will move in.

Six weeks ago, after our mother's funeral, my sister
cleaned out the apartment, discovered
the battered, cardboard boxes she sets down now
on the blue bedspread: *Read*
everything. Mark anything you think
I'd want to know.

Morphine has dulled your ungentle
struggle. In the background as I read, the sound of your
breathing, a soup of slow bubbles
that fill and break. Your caregivers turn you
every two hours, drape me in shawls of solicitude.

Buzzers caw, bedpans clamor, day after day the sun
makes its reliable way across your bedspread: a life
forms around me here. Feet wrapped in the white
afghan my mother knit
all the years she sat in this chair, I read the letters
you saved, the journals
you kept, the words you wrote. My sister stops in
every few hours, my brother stays
away, the cart comes round mornings
and afternoons, brings me
the small biscuits and juice that were the highlights
of your ten year stay.

Reading, reading. Those years before memory, the years
before our fights, your silences.
All here. Every
echoing detail.

As I read – how to describe it? –
the bedspread still itself, yet
unfamiliar, the light

that falls across this blue spread
a light that holds
something unknown,
unseen until now:

> you tried

to hold onto
every living minute of my earliest days.

Our firstborn, the apple of our eye.

The man in these pages,
dressed

> in your words,

a man I am meeting for the first time.

Your breaths foreground now,

> ragged,

> > the spaces between them

> > shadows

> > > that lengthen and lengthen.

The tearing of your

> final breaths.

This light.

November 2nd Dinner at My Sister's

It was autumn when we left home,
the leaves a welter of intense colour,
the clouds changing shades of bone
on silver white. By the time we reached
my sister's, two hours north-west by car,
it was winter, dervish spikes of snow
whirling across the road, the fields
a long white dream of fading light
lifting into distance and beyond.

We were seven at table that evening,
family, deeply familiar to one another,
in our fifties all, just beginning
to measure the time we had left and
find it wanting. My sister had dressed
her table in linen and set it with fine
china. We ate turkey and dressing and
root vegetables, drank *Château
Neuf de Pape*, talked of the old days.

My sister revealed that our mother
once killed a groundhog with an ax,
trapped it in the back porch and
hacked it to death. My brother told
that our father once killed a snake

---

barehanded, pulled
its head and its tail in opposite
directions 'til the long narrow body
came apart in the middle.

My sister served chocolate and
more wine. The ivory candles cast
shadows, limbs bent closer to the
house, harsh silver petals tapped
on the window. A sharp refrain,
my heart, these stories I had not
known, the hidden stars, our history
blown about the yard, a long moan
in fir, snow rewriting the contours.

Christmas Snow

The God of the Old Testament is arguably the most unpleasant character in all fiction.

Richard Dawkins

But that Sunday close to Christmas when I opened
the drapes wide, I saw Yahweh in a good mood for once,
his long horned toes curled around
a bar of cloud, broad hands holding and shaking out
a feather tick. The tick flapped up and down, up and down
and the sound was of a grand, far off
hullabaloo. God shook that old tick
the way my mother shook ours each spring,
sending a flurry of lackadaisical feathers into the farmyard,
feathers that were softer and more silky
than anything I've touched since.
                                     I'd been longing
for my mother that Christmas, though ten years had passed
since she died and I felt myself too old
for such behavior. I remembered
how we'd beaten and fluffed and fattened that tick
'til it puffed from the bed like new bread or new snow,
how that night long ago I slept on
feathers and air,
flew my long hollow bones over the dark spring fields,
the thin winding glitter of creek, the swamp,

---

its deafening sobsong of frogs.

                     All I knew then
was the little life of that house, that barn,
those cattle and pigs and sheep,
the shepherd God who counted the ninety-nine,
and went back for the one who was lost.

The Afterlife of Ashes

*With you I can imagine a place where to be phosphate of calcium
is enough.*

John Berger

When my husband told me he planned to leave
money in his will for our daughters
to travel to Machu Picchu
and in that high place of floating mists and dark
hillsides and ancient spirits
to scatter his ashes,
or rather when I learned this by overhearing him
talk about it with one of our daughters,
I said nothing, only absorbed,
through a long rainy season
where large light-filled drops hung oblong
from spoons and mirrors,
the knowledge that this was what he wanted,

then began to consider where my own bones would lie,
and with whom,

and eventually,
asked my sister if I could go in the grave
with her, and she said fine
but she'd have to ask

her husband, and he said he couldn't imagine
a better way to spend eternity
than *à trois* with her and me.

I thought, then,
of my husband's ashes –
dandruff on the shoulders of tourists,
irritants in the ears of llamas –
how, when they came to rest, it would be against
the hard silence of stones,

and I wept at last.

Not One Blossom

If I were to say that on a certain April Sunday afternoon
       of my sixty-third year,
when my husband was absent and my friends away

and I was in the garden moving a forlorn stone here,
       transplanting a drooping
fern there, that on this afternoon, a man I barely knew

pulled up at the garden gate in a white convertible
       with the top down
and invited me out, if I were to say that this was

the first time I had ever ridden in a convertible, and that
       though I have a fetish
about protecting my hair, I tossed it over my shoulder

and allowed a roar of wind to take it, like any blond
       movie star of twenty,
that the man took me to a cherry dell to sit upon a bench

beneath the cherry hung with bloom, you might say
       that this was a fairy tale,
and if I were to say that light played across the petals

---

and fluted through bee hum, that words drifted between us
 like fragrance, that a long
branch above us exhaled perfume and gently touched

my crown, that as we sat there, the day held its breath
 and not one blossom fell,
you might say – yes, a fairy tale. And yet,

I have told here the this-really-happened kind of truth,
 and moreover, I once said
to my sister that I dislike Sunday afternoons

because nothing ever happens on a Sunday afternoon.

Billy Collins Interviewed Onstage at Chautauqua

Billy Collins says you can't have people in your poems.
It can only be you and your reader.
You think of all the people in your poems:

your Aunt Evelyn, your sister, your friends Linda
and Dick and Ross. John Porter.
Your mother. Your mother. Billy Collins says

your job as poet is to give your reader pleasure.
Giving pleasure has always meant
one thing to you – sex. And your reader's crotch

is the one thing you never worried about. Billy Collins says
sometimes he takes his penis off
when he writes a poem. You wonder what his penis does

when it knows its master is writing. Goes to bars? Appears
for Margaret Atwood
as a remote-signature pen? Billy Collins says strangers

don't care about your thoughts and feelings. You want
to put up your hand, tell him about Adam,
who wanted to fix your car for nothing on a washed-up

Sunday afternoon in Ayton, Ontario. But Billy Collins is back
on pleasure. He says
how you give your reader pleasure is form. Dusty old **form**!

Grade ten sticking-to-your-varnished-wooden-seat iambic
pentameter! You're still mulling that
when Roger Rosenblatt asks Billy Collins why he didn't

become a jazz musician. Billy Collins says he wishes he **had**
become a jazz musician,
he wouldn't have to be on stage answering these questions.

So much for that egg-over-easy persona of the poems, eh?
Now he's saying no decent poet
ever knows the ending of a poem he's composing. You think

sadly of all those endings you thought of in the shower,
even though you know
you shouldn't use an adverb in a poem, even in a thought

about a poem. Then Roger Rosenblatt asks Billy Collins:
What is the importance of poetry?
Billy Collins sits up straight and says, *Poetry is optional.*

That's right, reader. Billy Collins, former Poet Laureate
of the United States of America
is sitting here on stage saying poetry is optional. And you

always thought people died for lack of what is found there.
Wait a minute. Something's happening
on stage. Billy Collins is donning his wings – they're

detachable, like his penis, I guess. There he goes – rising,
rising, riding the currents
of institutionalized sublimity. Billy Collins has the wingspan

of a frigatebird. Beating his defiant way across the ceiling,
beneath the track lighting,
brushing the Stars and Stripes aside. He's off to find

his roving mojo. You sigh and think about going home.
You'll have to rub out
all those people in your poems. You'll have to have a cold

shower whenever you feel an ending coming on.
You think sadly –
okay, adverbially – about your Aunt Evelyn.

How much
you loved her. How proudly she wore her moustache
to church.

Acknowledgements

Thank you, Marty Gervais and Black Moss Press.
Your support during the past six years has allowed me to
grow as a writer and has enriched my life. Thank you to
your talented team of editors and designers, who worked
long hours to transform the manuscript into a book:
Frances Boyd, Sheena Brennan, Phylmarie Fess, Kaitlyn
Fox, Kyle Hanemaayer, Hannah Larking, Snjana Leitao,
Chelsie Marie Pritz, Daniele Raymond, Laura Reisch,
Brandon Sabourin, Veronica Sinnaeve, Stephanie Small,
Luke Strople, Melyssa Tari.

Thank you to the *Literary Review of Canada*, *The
New Quarterly*, *The Antigonish Review*, *Grain*, *Prairie Fire*,
the *Windsor Review* and *Descant* where some of these
poems first appeared, in slightly different form. "Billy
Collins Interviewed Onstage at Chautauqua" was awarded
Descant's Winston Collins Best Canadian Poem prize of
$1,000 on February 20, 2009.

Thank you to the Second Cup of Westdale Village,
where this book was written. Thank you to John B. Lee.
To the OAC. To Don McKay for that time of privileged
temporality. To the Hamilton Poetry Center: Ross Belot,
Dick Capling, Jeffery Donaldson, Linda Frank, Bernadette
Rule, John Terpstra, Frances Ward, and members of
the big workshop. To J. S. Porter, who knows what book I
need before I do, and brings it to my door. To the writers

I've taught, and learned from, through the McMaster Certificate of Writing Program. To my weekly writing group: Ross Belot (to whom I owe the Collins penis as remote signature pen line), Dick Capling and Linda Frank. I single out Linda Frank. Her eye and ear are formidable. These poems and this book owe a big debt to her. For their love, and their support of my writing, I thank as well Julie Berry, Larry Cerson, Amy Dennis, Adam Getty, Sheila Gamble, Odile Gear, Teresa Kerr, Kathy May, Margaret McBride, Norma McDowell, Mary Ann Mulhern, Rae Rowbotham, The Keeds, and my daughters.

For Dan Pilling, Marie Gear Cerson and Tim McKergow: no words of thanks could ever suffice.

About the Author

Marilyn Gear Pilling lives in Hamilton, Ontario. Her first two books were collections of short fiction published by Cormorant and Boheme. She teaches poetry, belongs to several poetry workshops, and is currently president of the Hamilton Poetry Centre. She has recently completed a manuscript of creative non fiction, and is working on a collection of linked stories. All three genres of her work have won or been shortlisted for national contests.

Other books published by Black Moss Press:

The Field Next to Love (2002)
The Life of the Four Stomachs (2006)
Cleavage: A Life in Breasts (2007)

Marquis Book Printing Inc.

Québec, Canada
2009